The Struck Leviathan

with Strong winds from the
South Middle part calm —
latter part strong winds from
the North ship under all
sail standing to the N B W
saw a ship a boiling Sounds
in 55 fathoms of water Lat 45 —

Tuesday Jan 20th Commences with
strong winds from the North
latter part Calm first part
stood to the N S W at 6 PM
saw the land to no — whales
latter part Stood to the
S _ fresh wind in 45 12

Wednesday Jan 21th 1829 Commences with
strong winds from the North
steering to the E S E in company
with the Criterion of Nantucket
600 bbls of oil all of these 24 hours
saw no whales at 8 A M spoke
the Ship Hesper of Stonington

The Struck Leviathan/Poems on *Moby Dick*

John Bennett

A Breakthrough Book · University of Missouri Press, Columbia

The verso illustrations for this book are from the logs of
whaling voyages of Arthur Cox, Master of the ship *George and Martha*
of New Bedford, 1828–1829; ship *George and Martha* of New Bedford,
1829–1830; ship *Amazon* of New Bedford, 1830–1832. Courtesy
of the G. W. Blunt White Library, The Marine Historical
Association, Incorporated, Mystic, Connecticut

Library of Congress Card Number 70–130668
Printed in the United States of America
University of Missouri Press, Columbia, 65201   ISBN 0–8262–0099–0

For Warren Taylor, who persuaded me to
sign Ship's Articles / for Kiffin Rockwell,
who supplied a baron of beef / for Chad Walsh,
who blessed a voyage / for Henry Pochmann, who
read the Log / and for Elizabeth Bennett,
who could toll an Ahab home from sea.

The Devins Memorial Award

The Struck Leviathan won, in manuscript, the Devins Memorial Award for 1970. A provision of the Award—the major prize of the Kansas City Poetry Contests—is publication by the University of Missouri Press.

John Bennett's manuscript was chosen from more than three hundred collections submitted anonymously by poets across the nation.

The Award is made possible by the generosity of Dr. and Mrs. Edward A. Devins. Dr. Devins is former President of the Kansas City Jewish Community Center and is a patron of the Center's American Poets Series.

Contents

Ishmael: *Loomings, Christmas Day, Late*

The *Pequod*'s bows, vindictive, blunt with doom,
appareled with the jawbones of dead whales,
drove eyeless eastward into her sea room.
She caught the night wind in her thrumming sails
then slanted southward on the vague sea trails

far past Nantucket where the hungry dark
devoured the circles of eternity,
and Ahab braced himself on his stumped mark
to schism blankness into agony
and prove him human to the alien sea.

Father Mapple: *On the Abyss of the Godhead*

Sweet Isaac, helpless near the bush,
felt flame start wildly on his skin:
God took that flame and cast it round
the greenleaf bush and hotly in
to save old Abraham from sin.

And then the Ram, the Holy Ram,
became Child's Holy Surrogate:
He burned within the burning bush
and made both God and Man elate
that They were Christ's Beginning State.

saw the Land & 110 whales
latter part stood to the
So. Latitude in 45..12.

Wednesday Jan 21th 1829 Commences with
pleasant winds from the North
steering to the ESE. in company
with the Criterion of Nantucket
600 bbls of oil all of these 24 hours
saw no whales. at 8 AM spoke
the Ship Acasta of Stonington
1000 bbls of oil Latitude in 45.55

Thursday Jan 22d 1829 Commences with
calms latter part strong winds from
the North ship under all sail stands
to the East under all sail spoke the
Ship Eagle of New bedford 1600 bbls
in 46.17

Friday Jan 23d 1829 Commences
winds from the North Middle part
calm latter part like winds
from the No. first part stood
the East latter part to the So.

A Confirmed Landsman: *Looking out from Nantucket*

> The world's world and my own said *Damn the whales!*
> said *Damn the monsters in their tilting sea!*
> And so I chose a course which saves the skin
> that hides my bones, that holds my senses in
> so they might merge with Hume's sixth mystery
> and teach me how my doubled world prevails!

Father Mapple: *On Christ*

> The Fish in His Lovely Leaping
> drew light into the wave
> but Christ upon the cracked spars
> was Light the Godhead gave.

Tuesday Feb 10: 1829 All of these like winds
calms. Saw whales loward. the boats & got
hast & got one. boat stove & lost, the
whale. latter part saw a number
of whales. all hands. Employed in
boileing & repairing boats no Obs
96 fathoms of water

Wednesday Feb 11th 1829. Commences in
calms. latter part pleasant wind
from the SE saw many whale
but off the boats but could not
git fast. at e night finished
boileing latter part Employed
in stowing down. at 4. P.M. Spoke
the bark Alliance of Newport
80 bbls of oil 10 days out

Thursday Feb 12th 1829. All of these
SE Saw many whales. loward the
boats at 4. P.M. & killed one at 6. tes
him to the ship at 4. All went

Ishmael: *In the Crow's Nest*

At the ship's zenith close to heaven's depth,
the heavy boom of the bows comes faintly up
then fades through thin hysterias of wind
that mewl along the spars.

                                  I cling white-knuckled here.
Behind my eyes, coiled mysteries of height
beckon the sea to circles at my feet

                            or I
hang like a pendulum, dropped from the ship's deep root
down through the swing of the sky.

                                  I cling hard! hard!
to snaking lines lest I should slip and fall
straight upward through the empyrean clouds
or downward through the empyrean waves.

A German trap! A dreadful subtlety!

I call it losing self. I call it Death:
the Noumenon that Plato praised until
he drowned in honied cisterns of the mind.

I loose one hand, forcing the muscle and bone,
then gear me to the motion of this task
and live within my skin's circumference.

...... steering down. at 4. P. M. spoke
the bark Alliance of Newport
40 bbls of oil we days out —

Thursday Feb. 12th 1829. All of these
24 hours strong winds from the
S.E. Saw many whales lowered the
boats at 4. P. M. & kild one at 6 took
him to the Ship at 9. A.M. went
to cutting at 10 finished & went
to boileing set all sail to the
South —
Spoke the Schr brig Eff of
Stonington from the falklin islands
with 1500 skins. saw a windleward schr in
company did not learn her name. Lat 50.5

Friday Feb. 13th 1829. Commence
with lite winds & calms.

Father Mapple: *On the Resurrection*

> Betrayed by derelict autumn, the eft
> has burrowed below the possible light
> to clotted leaf slime and root vein, the weft
> of April abandoned, the dreadful night
> where efts sleep dark and cold until they come
> to newly risen April, that warm home.

Bulkington: *Musing at the Helm, Midnight*

From the strict rudder back toward shapeless gloom,
green fire lips and curls along the wake,
then fades to less than starshine on the waves.

Beneath the keel, the gliding Maldive sharks
act out the sea's assertion of the Word—
or partly some assertion of the Word—
while plankton, borne on wandering sea drifts,
act out that fiery pattern of the Word:
here I act out whatever *Yes!* I dare.

Tonight the sea sounds like a massive lung
breathing the sky. Dull thought! Where's chest or brain?
A bodiless lung that eats the wind? *BUT*:

the whale-filled veins of the sea, aye! shark-filled, God-filled,
and I, the fleeting observer, poised for a time
among brief shadows made of oak and flesh,
poised Oh! momently between the beginning and ending
that is my Beginning
                     was the Word
                                in the Beginning
was the Word and the Word was God.
'εν ἀρχῇ . . . my single tag of Greek translates to use!

Bulkington: *Later in the Same Watch*

The tiller moves, becomes less rigid than
the iron webs of mutability,
while I, my hands, its part and quick extension,
lend man salt to the sea salt of its turning.

Under the south wind, how the *Pequod* heels! heels!
and bends forever near and near
her final archipelagoes! The night,
like any night, grows deeply into dawn.

Those old stars touch this newer world with grace.

Sharks, whales, and men! all bearers of the Word:
and the Word endlessly falling through starlight and spindrift
or endlessly rising through waveshock and tiller
and the Word in the Beginning which is now the Infinite Now
and I myself, mortal, however It comes,
bearing the Word and affirming myself in the Word!

Dreaming my death, I become authentic Man.
Learning my death, I enter the dream of God.

Saturday June 13th 1829.

Commences with like winds from the
SE Ship under all sail standing to the
SW In latter part calm Employ
painting the Boats at 4 PM spoke
the Schooner Walkinger 16 day from
Shorgystone bound to Martinico
Latitude in by Obs _____ 34.18
Longitude in by account ____ 69.43.

Sunday = June 14th _____
Begins with Calms. Middle pleasant
winds from the SW Ship under
all sail standing to the West
Longitude in by account ___ 68.28
Latitude in by Obs ___ 35.48

Monday = June — 15th
Begins with plesant winds
from the South Middle & latter
part squally with showers

Ahab: *At His Cabin Window, Midnight*

This shackling cube! caged concentrate of space
borne rigidly above the swirling tides
that suck along the strakes and rudderpost!
Cribbed in this darkly pitching coffin, I
can watch my mind plumb through immensities,
through the chill malice of a universe
that Starbuck might no sooner learn to fear
than he did mother's milk!
                                Poor mooncalf! grown
brawny as oak, but in his ultimates
as flimsy as some village natural
that cucks and coos over an autumn leaf,
mistaking scarlet for a sign of joy!

I know what he can never dare to know:
by my hurt driven hard, I ram the voids,
denying them by ramming through them, thus!
and chart a godlike course.

                    No single sea
can float the keelson of my great intent:
the winds that rip that wavecurve into spume
are subject to my sail; and all the stars
that crack the firmament with frozen light
are merely points upon the private chart
that leads me circling back to my whole self!

Starbuck: *Variations on a Theme, Early Morning*

A fair fair day blooms down from this pure sky!
and eastward now, where light rides higher up,
the sweet hay cures beneath Andean slopes:
odours of earth and sunlight blown abroad
to sign a summer day on this bland sea.

I smell that magic here and lean at ease
over the lifting bulwarks, or I stand
locked warm in balance on the slanting deck,
my muscles, bones, blood, heart and brain attuned
to meet and marry glad reality.

The sea dazzles! Dazzles! What was the phrase?
Calm bridal? Aye, the young priest-poet, so!
but here of sea and sky.

                                    Like summer wind,
sunlight is melody. I hear it sing,
and through my beating heart, I also hear
the rhythmic providence that sets the world
on starry voyagings.

Damn sharks and men!
Damn Ahab's crazy feud! His cracked brain skews
one-hundred-eighty full degrees from true!
I look far down at what appalls him most,
I look far down, far down, and still I know
that this soft woman's motion in the sea
tells better truth than any truth he dreams
of that poor, dumb, hurt brute that razeed him!

Aye, like summer wind, sunlight is melody.
But sharkish men hear nothing in their heads,
and life can yield small profit or delight
till we grace eastward, home to Bedford wharves
and all that counters damned contrarieties!

all sail standing to the War she [?]
longitude in by account 68.28
Latitude in by Obs 35.48

Monday – June – 15th

Begins with Plesant winds
from the South Middle & latter
part squally with showers
of rain ship standing to the
W N by W   latter part bound
the ship in the Gilf Streame
saw a Brig standing to the
SE. Longitude by account 69.19
Latitude in by account – 39.28

Tuesday June – 16th

Begins with strong wind from the
S W ship under all sail standing
to the W W latter part wind
from the north set all sail to the
west   longitude in by account 70.45

Stubb: *As Usual*

Distrust the Whale? The helpful Whale?
Why, no! he'll soothe my grumpled gut!
Bring him beneath the flensing blade
and let the blanket piece be cut
and let the lower steaks be flayed
and fiercely broiled that I might eat!
On earth or sea no surer meat
can harden up a flaccid gut!

Fedallah, there, that wrinkled cod!
obeys a crazy Ramadan
and starves to feed a hungry god:
it's never struck his tiger brain
that whalemeat makes a better man
in ways a man had better be
once he has left the loveless sea,
nor that a man, once he's ashore,
must quickly rise for maid or whore!

Let gods or devils listen hard
to hear some falter in my pulse,
and let them know my given word's
"Fry whales in Hell—if nowhere else!"

Friday October 23 - 1829

Begins with like winds from the W &
ship under all sail standing to the South
the part strong gales from W
ship under short sail at 10 A M took
in the Waste Boats saw many fowl.
the water a dark greene ——————
Longitude in By Chronometer.   38.00.00
Latitude in By Obs. . . .   36.39

Saturday Oct 24 th

Begins with strong winds from the N W & ship
under short sail standing to the S W By S
Middle & latter part strong winds from the W Sa
t 6. A M set all sail to the S S E saw many
finBacks at 11 A M saw two rite whales. took in
sail headed to the S S E saw many Birds of all
kinds & the water a lite Collor ——————
Latitude in By Obs at 12.   38-18.
Longitude about   38° 00.00 By Chro

Sunday Oct

Bulkington: *The Struck Leviathan*

Like stoats that dare their own death if they hope
to sip at murdered veins, the whaleboats crept
with cunning lust across the heave to slope
where sea and air thrust flowing alternates.

Among the plankton sun tides where he slept,
the vivid lances woke the dreaming beast
to lunge and agony. His great flukes swept
a tumbled sea through roils to crimson yeast.
The iron rived his heart with alien gates
while overhead the mindless sea birds danced
a phantom woe upon the spinning air.

Oh! mourn the gallied whale whose death advanced
as he lay dreaming in his sunny lair!

under short sail standing to the S W By S
Middle & latter part strong winds from the w
at 6 AM set all sail to the S.S.E saw many
finbacks at 11 AM saw two rite whales took in
sail headed to the S.S.E saw many Birds of all
kinds & the water a lite Collor

    Latitude in By Obs at 12.   38-18.
    Longitude a Bout   38. 00.00 By C

Sunday Oct 25th 1829

All of these 24 hours strong gales from the
W S W ship hove to under the Maine
topsail & staysails headed to the South
at 6 AM wore to the N & on to set
a reefed foresail first part saw a
number of rite whales say 10 or 15 the
water a dark greene & many small
whale Birds at 4 Bell By Chron 38.0
    Latitude in at 12 By Obs.   38.

Whales all Headed to the N
not going fast

A Disgruntled Calvinist in Starbuck's Boat: *Sotto Voce*

By God! and yes, by God! and no, by God!
—and Starbuck's pride becomes the flesh of prayer!
In his damned poise and gesture, there he stands
over the smoking whale rope and speaks quick
idiot words that murder consequence!
If that line grabs him as the whale draws down,
he'll break in two as easy as boiled cod!

The shark's rough tooth, the sea's cold hug are what
Starbuck calls up with that child's mouth of his!

By God! and yes, by God! and no, by God!
—I'll tell him what it is that God would do:
He'd string us by our heels on blubber hooks
and flense the screaming fat from our cracked bones!

By God! and yes, by God! and no, by God!
—if Starbuck dares to name that Name again
before we're safe on deck, I'll show him God:
I'll ram his nose in whale scum, so! so! so!
and split his rigid arse with my toed boot!

Thursday - Oct. 29th 1829

All of these 24 hours strong gales from the
SE to ruged Employed in Boileing first par
ted to the SW middle part under short
sail headed to the South at 6 PM shoake the
ship Gen Porter with one whale ——

     Latitude in By Obs   34°,58′

———————————————————————————

Friday. Oct. 30th 1829.

All of these 24 hours strong gales from the
SE ship under short sail headed to the
South first part Employed in Boileing
at 6 PM stopt Boileing at 6 AM set
the tryworks to going But very ruged
saw many fowl the water a like
greene   no. Obs

———————————————————————————

Saturday Oct. 31 — 1829

Commences with strong gales from the SE ship
under short sail headed to the SE.
To Employed in Boileing at 10 night finishes

A Young Whaleman: *At His First Kill*

All strengths diminish here, all fail,
all shatter, dying through the sea:
the floating butchershop I serve
has taught me my mortality,

has taught me that the death I give,
the death that blinds the Zodiac
and eats great whales—flesh, bone, and brain—
sits vulture-beaked on my own back.

Ishmael: *High on the Mizzen Shrouds, He Remembers Them*

Tolled up toward leafy frequence
the golden tree frogs come
from the harsh moulds of winter
to celebrate the sum
of ponds spilled wide through Berkshire
with green light on green scum
with tadpoles quick to sequence
with dragonfly hum.

the tryworks to going But very ruged
saw many fowl the water a lite
greene no Obs

Saturday Octr 31 1825
Commences with strong gales from the SE ship
under short sail headed to the SE
Employed in Boiling at 10 night finished
latter part more moderate set all sail
to the NNE went to stowing
down at 10 AM saw a large sperm
Whale took chase But could not git
fast at 6 AM spoake the ship
Mercator of New Bedford one whale
Latitude in By Obs   36 . 05

H Sunday Novm 1 1825
these 24 hours lite winds & variable first part
saw six whales could not git fast so the
kild one & took it to the ship Employed
in cuting Latitude in 38 . 20 Long 38 24

A Frightened Whaleman: *On Deck During a Storm*

> The *Pequod* rams her blunted bow—
> that stupid fist of tarry oak—
> down through the greyly surging seas
> and smashes water into smoke.
>
> The blubber fools who watch that spume
> and take its making as their own
> will learn another kind of thought
> when they and ship are overblown
>
> and sucked down through the hungry seas
> which rise to eat that staggered bow,
> that stupid fist of tarry oak
> whose ramming strength they worship now!

A Ribald Boy/Man: *The First Forecastle Song*

Sweet Nancy of Hilo,
she's wild as a shark,
she yaws like a whaler
when she sails the dark!
          Blow, blow, blow the man down!
          Oh! take me to Hilo and ease the man down!

The captain's gone crazy
from drinking on shore,
the mates have deserted,
a-chasing some whore!
          Blow, blow, blow the man down!
          Oh! take me to Hilo and ease the man down!

The oil casks grow rancid,
the bilge pumps, they fail,
and there's no sailors left
to work the topsail!
          Blow, blow, blow the man down!
          Oh! take me to Hilo and ease the man down!

Sweet Nancy of Hilo,
she's built like a bark,
I'll climb up her scuppers
and sail through the dark!
       Blow, blow, blow the man down!
       Oh! take me to Hilo and ease the man down!

I'll climb up her scuppers
and sail her full fair,
and when I drop anchor
she'll know I been there!
       Blow, blow, blow the man down!
       Oh! take me to Hilo and ease the man down!

Saturday Nov.r 14 th 1823

All of these 24 hours strong winds from
the North Ship under Short sail Employ
in Boileing at 4 Morning finished at 6
A M went to Stowing down latter part
showers of rain saw many finbacks
& c — O.b.

Sunday Nov.m 15 th 1823 —

H Begins with strong winds &
rainy latter part lite winds
& variable at 1 P.M saw one whale off. Boats
kild him at 4. P.M took it to the ship at
6. P.M finished cutting at 6 morning went to
Boileing saw a ship to the East name not no
saw many finbacks no Obs

Monday Nov.r 16 th 1823

Begins with lite winds from the S.E latter part
strong winds from the East at 12 night finis

Bulkington: *The Far Shore*

> The North Star drains
> from the Dipper's edge,
> the sea drains back
> at the Moon's command,
> the wind blows over
> the broken sedge,
> the hurt fish drowns
> on the mottled sand.

Tasting Sea Spray, An Irish Whaleman Gains His Joke

> As salty—be damned! and Billy-be-damned!
> —as good pig meat that the mineral turns!
> Where in the name of Christ-over-me
> grew all of this wet salt the dry land spurns?
>
> One single taste and the tongue coils back
> and the mind coils even further!
> I'd swear that the rivers that drown in the sea
> hold the salt salt blood of all murther,
>
> hold the hurt blood sucked from the veins of man
> since the world was dissolved into terror:
> be-damn-bho! I'll never taste it again!
> It's a moral and chemical error!

Ishmael: *The Pod*

Under soft sunlight
on the glinting tides
the gentle sea beasts roll
in love or loving play.

Those children of salt time—
those bulls whose greatly muscled sex
would cause the Bull to stare,
those cows whose filling wombs make birth
the absolute of love,
those calves whose innocence hurls them
through tides of hugest joy—
those tons of flesh are gentle as the kiss
that other lovers give.

The halcyon sea and its great beasts are one:
God's holy purpose, single, multiform,
defines a joyous image of itself.

Pip: *Song for His Lost Self*

The tomb is sea enough to float us all.
I drown at God's left hand and call
      fal de ral
      fal de ral de rollio.
Small waves to roaring oceans grow.
Where hides the sun? Sing fast and slow
      fal de ral
      fal de ral de rollio.
Some carelessness in whose hand let
me plunge from dry worlds into wet?
I am turned ague now, and pale
as that dread whiteness of the Whale.
      Sing *fal de ral*
      fal de ral de rollio.
Once I lived stranger to the shark:
we draw together here. This dark
is both my sickness and my shroud.
The sea shells in my brain boom loud:
      fal de ral
      fal de ral de rollio.

kild him at 4. P.M. took it to the ship at —
... A.M. finished cutting at 6 morning went to
Boiling saw a ship to the East name not known
saw many finbacks _____ no Obs ___

Monday. Nov.r 16th 1829

Begins with light winds from the S.E. latter part
Strong winds from the East at 12 night finish
Boiling at 6. A.M. set all sail to the S.W.
t' went to stowing down. saw many finbacks
first part latter part saw some rite
whales. loward the Boats & took one to
the ship Latitude in By Obs. 39.52
Longitude By Chron.m   40. 52. 15

H Tuesday. Nov.m 17th 1829.
Begins with strong winds from the Ea-
middle part moderate latter part strong
winds from the S.W. ship under short sai-
headed to the South first part Employ
in Cutting latter part in Boiling & stowing do-

Ishmael: *At His First Cutting-In*

In God's name, who can see the Whale entire?
Who name him in his great entirety?
Preponderant, that flesh has whelmed my sight!

My quarrel with God is that He gave me less
of eye and tongue than I find needful here.
I'd *see* the Whale and *name* him and so give
Creation back to Its Exultant Source
whose best exultance is man's joy in It!

Ahab: *His Vision of the Kraken*

Where green-skulled whalemen lie, where no tides run,
deep down and dark in that unsculptured gloom,
the great sea squid gropes blindly unaware
of lean Egyptians drowned in spicy rock
or Capricorn knocked hornless in the east,
a blare of goatcry shaking constellations.

Deep down and dark where mudbones gird the world,
by arm and sucking arm and sucking arm,
a polyp blob creeps through the heavy depths
where Satan, homeless, might establish home.

The Old Manxman: *Splicing a Line by Lantern Light*

Beyond the pitching mast, Orion strides
around the Southern Pole! the *Pequod*'s bow
nudges his crotch in the upsweep, then
falls off to leeward in the western wind.

Ah, there's a catching thought some fancyman
would like to learn! Should poisoned Flask come up
to see that vision from these bucking planks,
he'd have hard words for poor Daggoo tomorrow. . . .

No. No! Damn hell! Both man and thought are death,
a deathly match to match the shark-filled sea!
Eaters of men.
                    But Pip's a holiness.

I am too old, too dull, have fallen long
through equinoctial houses and their signs. . . . I lose
what sense I had of where. . . . Was it the Bull or Crab?
The Fishes or the Scales?

                    Well, Stonehenge, then.
   Could I remember what my father said
   of what his father's father had received
   from generations back. . . . I lose all sense
   of Time, of Space in Time! Could I recall
   exactly why the ancient priestly ones
   set up the circled stones all pointing so,
   there past sweet Man behind the English coast,
   I'd braid a pattern in this druid line.

   Let be. Let be. The world is surely round,
   and we sail out to come full circle in it:
   all motion rests on Stonehenge or the Whale,
   no matter how obscurely.

                    Let be! Let be!
   A thought can measure zero, nothing more.
   Log lines, spliced tight, must measure even less.

Stubb: *In Private, Oddly Sullen and Thoughtful*

What does he want? What should a ship become,
bearing a Starbuck out of Bedford Town?
A floating seaman's bethel? Or a home—
GOD'S HOME, of course—a seasick altar sent
to bring to knee the watered firmament
with great sea eagles shackled and brought down?
Sharks set to prayer? The huge whales all subdued,
dressed greyer than they are, dressed greyer-hued?

A man who has his skill with lance or boat,
who keeps a rope from kinking on the post—
hell, he's as good, he's better yet than most!
Why should he then want churches sent afloat?
Want men at prayer when they have oars to work
or flukes to stay apart from? Why should he
make every act a stiffened piety?

Something's gone wrong in him. I'd swear it's so.
A rigid kind of wrong. No mortal man,
though he be godly, comes upon the sea
and hopes to tell the winds how they can blow.
He'd parse a text or cite a homily
right in the middle of a harpoon throw
if any listened. His men won't. And now
he uses silence as a sermon.
                              Christ!
I think that whales are oil, no more, but he
would say God's blessing makes horizons bend.
Well, so it might—or then, so it might not.

And ambergris is whaleshit in the end.

H Sunday Novʳᵐ 22 1829.
H Begins with lite winds, from
the SW ship under all sail
standing to the wⁿE at 3 Pᵐ saw
two rite whales lowared the Boats to kild them
Both at 6 Bell took them to the ship latter part
lite winds from the East at 6 Bell went to
cutting at 11 finished Cuting frot at 12. 38.49

Monday Novʳᵐ 23ᵈ 1829
All of these 24 hours. Strong winds from
the East to the norⁿE. at 1 Pᵐ
saw whales lowared the Boats & struck.
kild & sunk the Whale los 2 Sharts of line
took up the Boats & went to Boileing at
6 Bell saw a whale lowared the Boats
could not git fyes t at 9 lowared struck
& parted the line lost 2 Sharts. ship under
Short Sail Rankit in By ﬁﬁ 39. 04

A Whaleman Sings It: *The Second Forecastle Song*

Sweet was my brother, sweet was his voice,
sweet was his youth—but the wild flukes tossed!
The stove boat dragged him down through the sea:
my brother drowned, my brother was lost!

> *Sing woe! woe! throw the man down,*
> *throw him to Hell and teach him despair;*
> *teach him to walk below the waves,*
> *teach him to breathe that heavy air!*

My brother went down to the still still dark,
my brother went down because he was man;
my brother went down beneath the whale
and choked and died and cried "I am!"

> *Sing praise! praise! raise the man up,*
> *raise the man up and give him to light,*
> *raise him up from the cold cold sea*
> *and give him the joy of his pure sight!*

Ahab: *Near the Mainmast, Sunrise*

Into this madman horror of the sun
how many men crawl forth reluctant now
from the grey swamps of sleep and dress themselves
in clothes that stink with mortal yesterdays?

Cursed endless *batter! batter!* wind and wave!
bows crashing down, green water surging up,
and the long, whining dip of mast and spar!

Who truly listens on this ship? Who hears?
Across the fronts of heaven, silence grows
between the muted thunder of old suns
like some enormous cancer;
                              here, the sea
roars out its manic scansion, pauses, beats,
lifts to crescendo scream, and then drops down
through seething voids that drain my outraged heart
of its warm rhythms.

                 Soon! Soon! Oh! Soon!
that blunt-faced phantom from the shrouded depths,
that damned razeeing bastard devil brute
whose rending jaw cut coldly at my quick
will rise to meet me on the upper seas!

In what last tide or precinct of my course
will he breach forth to learn that I can kill?
No matter where he hides, no matter where!
I'll chase him out across the compass rose,
through every strait and passage of the sea!
I'll chase him round the Maelstrom's triple lip
and round the brimming flames of Hell itself
until my lance drives down through his heart's root!

Come, Moby Dick! My compliments to ye!
My compliments, my very best to ye!
I bear a gift of tempered steel whose edge,
baptized with blood almost as wild as yours,
will force ye to attend me when we meet
and grave sweet lessons on your sullen heart!

Come, Moby Dick! Come, Moby Dick! Come! Come!

the East to the over.d. at 1 P.M
saw whales lowerd the Boats & struck
kild & ssunk the Whale los 2 Shots of line
took up the Boats & went to Boileing at
6. A.M saw a whale lowerd the Boats
Could not git fast at 9. lowerd & struck
& parted the line lost 2 shots. ship under
Short Sail Nantucket in By Obs_ 39, 04

Tuesday. Nov.r 24 th 1829.
Begins with Strong winds from the eward
latter part wind from the North &c.
first part Employed in Boileing at 6 A
stopt Boileing on account of the rain
saw a number of rite whales & many
finBacks. no Obs

Wednesday. Nov.m 25 th 18__
Begins with Strong winds fr
the S & W ship under
short sail Employed in Bo
at 8 A saw whales of Boats

Ishmael: *He Imagines Concatenation*

A coil of whale guts rotting through the sea:
the primal order of epiphany.

Tuesday — Dec.r 22th 1829

All of these 24 hours strong gales from
the N.o W.t squally ship under short
sail at 1 P.M. saw a rite whale
off Boats struck & drew the iron
Latitude in By Obs. i. — 40.02

Wednesday Dec.r 23d 1829

All of these 24 hours strong gales
from the N.o W.t ship under short
sail lying to took in the waist Boat
saw a number of rite whales
Latitude in By Obs... 40.08
Longitude in By Chron. 36. 45

Thursday — Dec.r 24th 1829

First part strong winds from the S.o W.t
latter part calm saw many finbacks
Imployed in repairing a marine ....
Latitude in By Obs. 39.58

Friday Dec.r 25th 1829

A Whaleman Murmurs It, Watching the Sunrise

Christ have mercy upon us!

Deep down deep down where water falls asleep,
the blind and subtle sea worms multiply
simplicities of bone;
                    they shyly wait
for good that falls upon them from their sky
of heavy tides.

Lord have mercy upon us!

Blind mouths!
                Blind mouths!
                              A slow devouring,
deep in the secret places where we fall
forever lost to light, the sweet, sweet light!

Poor mortal flesh! Poor doomed and damned! We go
to endings that our mothers never meant
when we came squalling from that better dark!

Christ have mercy upon us!
Lord have mercy upon us!
Christ have mercy upon us!

Latitude in Bg Obs........................... 40.08
Longitude in Bg Chron........................ 36.45

Thursday — Decm 24th 1823.
First part Strong winds from the SW
Latter part — Calm saw many finbacks
Employed in repairing a marine topsail
Latitude in Bg Obs.......................... 39.58

Friday Decm 25th 1823 — | |

B. H Begins with lite winds
from the West at all sail
to the North at 4 PM saw many rite
whales off Boats struck one & drew the iron
struck one moer at 10 night got it
to the ship at 4 AM went to
cutting at 9 AM finished & went to
Boiling at 10 spoke the ship
George of Nantucket — 150 bbls of oil
Sellen a number of finbacks
Latitude in Bg Obs.......................... 39.35

Bulkington: *Obliteration and Transcendence*

The fading susurration of the blood
in those great arteries: imagine it!
The subtle life of brute and semifish
forgets its lunar rhythms, slows, slows, slows;
and the vast net of muscle, flesh, and brain
drops down to death before the ventricles
are truly stilled.
                  No slightest tremor moves
between the thousand thousand billion cells
there lying spent upon the upper sea.

Like some dead god, the whale falls out of time—
or grows eternal, dying into time.

Ishmael: *Orphan Theme*

The dolphin, small sea-shouldering one,
took up the *Rachel*'s orphan son
and carried him upon the sea
until their days had numbered three

and when the third long day was done
the dolphin's sturdy body broke
and God dissolved them into one
beneath the sea wrack and sea smoke.

Tuesday Jan 26th 1830

H these 24 hours Moderate Breeses from the Wes

H at 6 PM saw two whales of Boats & kild them Boath at 12 night took them Boath to the Ship at 4 AM went to cuting no Cles

Wednesday Jan 27th 1830

All of these 24 hours lite winds & Thick weather at 4 PM finished cuting & went to Boiling latter part starting the Brecs into a State room saw a number of whales of Boats strock one & drew the iron saw one Ship name not known no — Cls

Thursday Jan 28th 1830

All of these 24 hours plesant winds from the North ship under short sail Employd in Boiling & Stowing down saw one whale of Boats couldnot git fast saw one Ship to the West hat By Obs 41.34

Fedallah: *Exultant, After the First Sighting*

Something deathly this way comes,
hidden by the shadowed wave.
Neither shark nor whale is He:
neither lance nor sail can save.

Ahriman in His Whale Shape
comes to taste the sacrifice.
I must serve Him as He wills:
dooms of fire or of ice,

dooms of blood along the blade,
dooms of melding with the sea!
Ahriman the Dark God comes:
none so fierce and strong as He!

Let the foolish Christians learn,
and those other infidels,
that they never dared to dream
of true heavens or true hells;

no! nor learned the Cycle which
hurls Good beneath the Other Good
and endlessly resolves Itself
in sea and desert, plain and wood!

whales off Boats struck me & drew the
iron saw one Ship name not known
&o———— Obs

Thursday Jan'y 28th 1830
All of these 24 hours plesant winds from
the North ship under short sail Employed
in Boileing & stowing down saw one whale
if Boats couldnot git fast saw one
Ship to the West fat By Obs. 41.34

Friday Jan'y 29th 1830
Begins with strong winds from the East
ship under short sail headed to the & S.
& Employed in Boileing latter part stron gales
from the S.E. with raine at 4. P.M finished
Boileing &o B.B.

Saturday Jan'y 30th 1830
These 24 hours strong gales from the
Eastward ship under short sail Employd

Ishmael: *Death of Ahab*

Flesh-borne in whale, the world's blind windigoes
leapt forth to murder Ahab
                              AND! the sea,
grown prodigal with many coral dooms,
fell back from vortex into liturgy:
                    Men and their Final Angel meet
                    on curving wave, on level street:
                              Timor mortis conturbat eos.

On far green lands, the heavy cities rust
in careless sunlight
                              AND! beneath carved stones,
through crazy scatters of enormous dark,
the frightened dreamers hide unhinging bones:
                    Men and their Final Angel soon
                    meet in the dying afternoon:
                              Timor mortis conturbat eos.

Monday- Oct. 18th 1830

All of these 24 hours strong winds from the North by,
Course Ea't E' at 4 P.M. spoke the ship paciffic of Nantucket
whaler saw finBack.6 & many fowl of all kinds
Lat. 36 33

Tuesday- Oct. 19th 1830

All of these 24 hours plesant winds from the North
ship, by the wind to the Ea't E' saw many finbac
to th'd 35.43.   Lattitude By Chrom   7. 27/6

Wednesday. Oct. 20th 1830
All of these 24 hours. winds from the North
ship under all Sail Cours. Ea't E'. at 8 A.M
saw one rite whale off Boats & Sunk him
No   6 B 6

Thursday- Oct. 21th 1830
All of these 24 hours lite winds from the North
& plesant weather first part saw a number of rite
whales lowerd the Boats a number of times couldnt
rite boat latter part saw many rite boats

Ishmael: *Death of Flask*

Thinly beneath the shallow plankton gloom,
a squalling death's-head gapes behind lank hair;
briefly its face screams upward in the sun;
its thin lungs retch upon a gobbling breath;
membraned with fear like batwings, its clawed hands
gouge gouge their dread into a drowned man's back.

A joyless insolence becomes at last
its broken eyes, becomes a maggot's writhe
through death, then spirals down and down and down
through the black pelvic crush of undersea.

All of these 24 hours winds from the North
Ship under all Sail Cours Et E Cd St Ot
saw one rite whale off Boats & Sunk him
No

Sunk

Thursday — Oct. 21st 1830
All of these 24 hours lite winds from the North
& Plesant weather first part saw a number of rite
whales lowerd the Boats a number of times couldnt
git fast latter part saw many whales at 6 &c
off Boats & kild one and took it to the Ship
went to cuting took the head & lips found the
whale to be a dry skin cut away & stood to the
Eastward Lat # 35—09 Long 5°·00″ West

H Dry Skin

Broke &

Broke S   C Broke

H Friday Oct. 22 1830
All of these North first part saw
whales off Boats got fast to one & drew the iron
latter part saw whales off Boats & kild one that

Starbuck: *Accepting Death*

High in their shaken tower
the bells remembered God:
through the white clouds at Bedford
they sent His Name abroad

in my last last October
when leaves came twisting down
to lie in drift and bumble
upon the Sunday town.

Here in its yelping power
the wind grips ship and sail:
all other noise grows noiseless,
all distant towers fail

while teeth-tiered sharks glide lower
to taste the choking doom
where speechless God has entered
my last enormous room.

Broke

Dry Skin

Tuesday Decm 14th
These 24 hours Strong winds from the WSW to the West at 4 PM stove two whales to the Ship latter part Employed in Cutting found one whale to Be a dry skin so let her go saw a number of whales & one whale ship Lattitude in By Obs 38-53

Wednesday Decm 15th 1830
These 24 hours Strong winds from the NW Ox ship under short sail headed to the SofSW saw a number of whales these 24 hours Employ'd in Boiling & Stowing down oil &c

Thursday Decm 16th 1830
These 24 hours Strong Breezes from the WNW ship under short sail all hands Employed in Boiling & Stowing down saw a whale ship to the WSW

Ishmael: *'Pequod' Down*

After the whaleblow, atilt as in windcurve
then
poised on the round lip of vortex and shatter
then
the *Pequod* foundered in deep skirl of downpitch.

All of her bright men, caged in the maelstrom,
blossomed like flowers. And Tashtego opened
sunward his petals of laughter.

Sea wind whine, a curlew piping.
Fiercely the manforms broke dark waves to silver
and death cries were trumpets, were split-echo coral.

the Ward Ship under short sail headed to the S of W saw a number of whales these 24 hours Employed in Boiling & Stowing down oil &c ——

Thursday Dec'r 16th 1830

All of these 24 hours strong Breezes from the Ward Ship under short sail all hands Employed in Boiling & Stowing down saw a whale Ship to the Ward latitude in By Ob'g. 39.05

Friday Dec'r 17th 1830

All of these 24 hours strong winds from the Ward with fog Ship under short sail at 8 Pm finished Boiling latter part Employed in Stowing down

---

Saturday Dec'r 18th 1830

All of these 24 hours strong winds from the W & N with a thick fog Ship under short sail all hands Employed in Screwing whale Bone latitude in By Ob'g. 39.03.

here in By Chron'm with on the Meridian